To Mary

From Jean

IGNITING *the* SPARK *for*

YOUR NEXT GREAT ADVENTURE!

Run Like a Girl

KATHY VICK

HOWARD BOOKS

A Division of Simon & Schuster

New York London Toronto Sydney

Our purpose at Howard Books is to:
> *Increase faith* in the hearts of growing Christians
> *Inspire holiness* in the lives of believers
> *Instill hope* in the hearts of struggling people everywhere
> Because He's coming again!

Published by Howard Books, a division of Simon & Schuster, Inc.
1230 Avenue of the Americas, New York, NY 10020
www.howardpublishing.com

Run Like a Girl © 2009 by Kathy Vick

ISBN: 978-1-4165-8639-5

10 9 8 7 6 5 4 3 2 1

HOWARD and colophon are registered trademarks of Simon & Schuster, Inc.

Manufactured in China

For information regarding special discounts for bulk purchases, please contact: Simon & Schuster Special Sales at 1-866-506-1949 or business@simonandschuster.com.

Edited by Chrys Howard
Cover and interior design by LeftCoast Design, Portland, OR 97229
Cover Photo:
    Kid Millman, Getty Images
Interior photos and illustrations:
    Greg Whitaker (pp. 9, 26, 29, 44, 50, 54)
    Shutterstock (pp. 4–5, 10, 11, 12–13, 23, 33, 42, 46, 52)
    Getty Images (pp. 3, 6, 14, 31, 34, 35, 37, 38, 41, 49, 53)
    Veer (pp. v, vi)
    Fotosearch (pp. 19, 25)
    iStockphoto (pp. 12 *small*, 13 *small*, 16–17, 18, 20, 30, 39, 43, 45)

Dedication

To my husband, Pat,

who reminds me every day

that the world is waiting.

Introduction

For last year's words belong to last year's language and next year's words

await another voice. And to make an end is to make a beginning.

T. S. ELIOT, *Little Gidding II*

Long ago, your life lay before you like a limitless horizon. You couldn't then know all the turns, dips, and switchbacks your life would take. Today, you stand with a full view of where you have been, and a *new* horizon, and you are once again filled with a mixture of anticipation and uncertainty.

A familiar voice whispers, "There is something I have designed just for you." The voice has become louder and more frequent, and as you stand here, a part of you wants to reclaim the girl who saw herself as a force; another part of you is not sure that girl still exists.

Yet you sense that your life has led you here, and miraculously, you have landed exactly where you are supposed to be—the right place, and the right time. This is what gives you the courage to explore, laugh, reinvent, reclaim the girl who lives just beneath your skin—to listen to her, find your joy, *Run Like a Girl.*

I invite you to consider, for a moment, the girl in you. What is she saying? And what will you do when you find her?

Kathy Vick, Certified Life Coach

www.fluentlifecoaching.com • www.runlikeagirl.org

run like a girl

Before I shaped you in the womb,
I knew you, before you were
born, I set you apart.

JEREMIAH 1:5 NIV

If you surrendered to the air, you could ride it.

Toni Morrison

run like the swift river that flows to the sea,
run like the gazelle over the savanna,
run like the stars jetting across the sky.

When it's over, I want to say: All my life I was a bride married to amazement. I was the bridegroom, taking the world into my arms.

MARY OLIVER, *When Death Comes, New and Selected Poems*

Those who are wise will shine like the brightness of the heavens, and those who lead many to righteousness, like the stars forever and ever.

DANIEL 12:3 NIV

Oh man! There is no planet sun or star could hold you, if you but knew what you are.

RALPH WALDO EMERSON

*G*etting out of my car on a warm September afternoon in the mountains, I was swept back to the scent and color of my childhood in Central Oregon: juniper, fir, and pine trees paired with a landscape of gold, orange, copper, brown and green. Memories came alive; of a little girl framed in high desert and mountain air. A girl enchanted with school, autumn, running and playing in the foliage, hiding behind the juniper trees, making forts in the bushes —free with the wonder of life!

EVADNE WOODSIDE

Who can hold back a woman that knows who made her and for what?

When I was ten I ran bases with the other kids on our street. I was light and fast and not afraid of falling. We played until dark and our parents called us from the porches like shepherds across mountains. When I was twenty I ran across a big wooden floor, learning how to move without touching the ground. When I was thirty I ran from my marriage, because it had stopped cold, lost in a cul de sac.

When I was forty I ran from everything I knew to catch up to and keep my soul's friend in this life. Now I'll run against time's river, to see how far I can get up that stream.

TERRIE SHATTUCK

run toward the wide horizons, and the whispers of dreams.

Twenty years from now, you will be more disappointed by the things you did not do than by the things you *did* do. So throw off the bowlines. Sail away from the safe harbor. Catch the trade winds in your sails. Explore. Dream. Discover.

MARK TWAIN

When you have a dream, you've got to grab it and never let go.

CAROL BURNETT

"For I know the plans I have for you," declares the Lord, "plans to prosper you and not to harm you, plans to give you hope and a future."

JEREMIAH 29:11 NIV

It's the dream that you had at ten years old and still dream at fifty that you need to pay attention to.

run up the mountains of your imagination, and silence the voice that says: "You can't."

The possible's slow fuse is lit by the imagination.

EMILY DICKINSON

When Jesus said, "Woman, thou art loosed," He did not call her by name. He wasn't speaking to her just as a person. He spoke to her femininity. He spoke to the song in her. He spoke to the lace in her. Like a crumbling rose, Jesus spoke to what she could, and would have been. I believe the Lord spoke to the twinkle that existed in her eye when she was a child; to the girlish glow that makeup can never seem to recapture. He spoke to her God-given uniqueness. He spoke to her gender.

SERITA JAKES, *T. D. and Serita Jakes Speak to Women, 3-in-1*

I tell you the truth, if anyone says to this mountain, "Go, throw yourself into the sea," and does not doubt in his heart but believes that what he says will happen, it will be done for him.

MARK 11:23 NIV

What we think is possible is intricately connected to what our history tells us is true. Sometimes we need to rewrite that story.

*T*here's something satisfy-ing about that stringy little wisp of hair that gets stuck in your mouth when you're running. When I was a child, I remember racing through a field in a white flower-girl dress. It was weeks after the wed-ding, the bride was long gone, the guests had gone home, the tent was down, but the dress was going strong. With my heart racing, I put one scuffed, white, patent leather shoe in front of the other. The dande-lions became my audience; the wind my band. And those little pieces of soggy hair were proof that beauty isn't about appear-ance, it's about the experience.

LAURA SPEIDEL

What keeps you going isn't some fine destination but just the road you're on, and the fact that you know how to drive.

BARBARA KINGSOLVER

Racing is a matter of spirit not strength.

JANET GUTHRIE

Use what you have to run toward your best—that's how I now live my life.

OPRAH WINFREY

Do you not know that in a race all the runners run, but only one gets the prize? Run in such a way as to get the prize.

1 CORINTHIANS 9:24 NIV

You can tell a lot about a woman just by the way she walks into a room.

more than the finish line or the prize.

running is about God's intention and yours.

There are two ways to live your life. One is as though nothing is a miracle. The other is as though everything is a miracle.

ALBERT EINSTEIN

I do it for the joy it brings, cause I'm a joyful girl. 'Cause the world owes us nothing, we owe each other the world.

ANI DIFRANCO

I was thrust into your arms at my birth. You have been my God from the moment I was born.

PSALM 22:10 NLT

In all of us is a place of joy that we experience only when we are fully engaged in the business we were created for.

so, run for the joy of it!

When I smell the fragrance of fresh mowed lawn it takes me back to childhood memories of growing up on a seventy-acre, Ohio farm, meticulously cared for by my father. My brother and I were responsible for mowing our large lawn; each getting paid 75 cents for a hard day's work. When we were done, we'd kick off our shoes and run through the grass, playing until the sky filled with fireflies, blinking their bright little lights. By the time we went in for the night our feet would be stained brilliant green. No wonder the very smell of fresh cut grass makes me think of carefree childhood days, the joy of running with my brother and green feet.

KAY MADEIRA

run with the treasure that lies beneath your skin, run with permission to guard and keep it.

I've learned lately that no one is going to hand me a permission slip and tell me to take time out for me.

WYNONNA JUDD

The history of all times, and of today especially, teaches that . . . women will be forgotten if they forget to think about themselves.

LOUISE OTTO

But those who hope in the LORD will renew their strength. They will soar on wings like eagles; they will run and not grow weary, they will walk and not be faint.

ISAIAH 40:31 NIV

Just putting yourself on the list will change your life.

Ah, Hawaii! What an incredible place to run, play, and blossom. One of my fondest memories of growing up in paradise is the gift of fragrant flowers and the leis we made from them.

With my siblings years older than me and living on the mainland, the trees and their flowers became my friends. Not only were they there for me in their beauty and bounty, but I counted on them in ways that others could not. With each blossom that I chose for my mother's long lei needle, I grew happier with anticipation. For it was as I created this wondrous strand of frangipani, with its scent of heaven, that I found how much the graceful gift of the lei caressed my shoulders and gladdened the heart of this simple island girl.

NANI STEWART

On the beach—

the water could not

outrun me

even when it chased me

back toward the sand.

Because I felt the

strength of the sun

and

the wind and the waves,

and I

burst out laughing with

delight.

And that just made me

run faster.

LORE SHATTUCK

run with fierce conviction and resolute courage.

Courage doesn't always roar. Sometimes courage is the quiet voice at the end of the day saying, "I will try again tomorrow."

MARY ANN RADMACHER

When you have decided what you believe, what you feel must be done, have the courage to stand alone and be counted.

ELEANOR ROOSEVELT

When you get into a tight place, and everything goes against you, till it seems as though you could not hold on a moment longer, never give up—for that is just the place and time that the tide will turn.

HARRIET BEECHER STOWE

…Be strong and courageous. Do not be terrified; do not be discouraged, for the LORD your God will be with you wherever you go.

JOSHUA 1:9 NIV

 Our most courageous acts are often the ones we take for granted, knowing and accepting ourselves, working on our marriages, perhaps surviving a divorce, raising children. These acts rival David and Goliath.

17

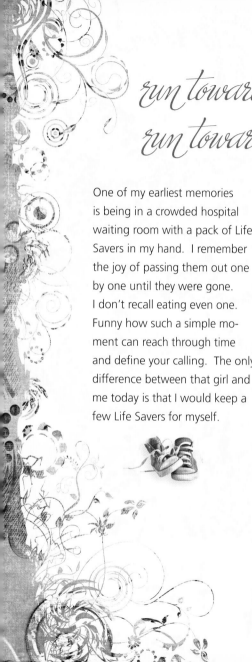

run toward those who are hurting; run toward those who comfort you.

One of my earliest memories is being in a crowded hospital waiting room with a pack of Life Savers in my hand. I remember the joy of passing them out one by one until they were gone. I don't recall eating even one. Funny how such a simple moment can reach through time and define your calling. The only difference between that girl and me today is that I would keep a few Life Savers for myself.

The greatest pleasure I know is to do a good action by stealth, and to have it found out by accident.

CHARLES LAMB

You have to treat people gently because we're all in a process. What might seem like a good idea to somebody at twenty-one is probably not going to seem like a good idea at fifty, but you don't know that until you get there.

AMY GRANT

As a mother comforts her child, so will I comfort you . . .

ISAIAH 66:13 NIV

run with forgiveness on your tongue,

No one deserves to live a life of unforgiveness. It will twist you up into a person you never intended becoming.

run to forgive yourself.

If we really want to love, we must learn how to forgive.

MOTHER TERESA

Do the kinds of things that come from the heart. When you do, you won't be dissatisfied, you won't be envious, you won't be longing for somebody else's things. On the contrary, you'll be overwhelmed with what comes back.

MITCH ALBOM,
Lessons from Tuesdays with Morrie

There is a time for everything...a time to scatter stones and a time to gather them...

ECCLESIASTES 3:1–5 NIV

Life appears to me too short to be spent in nursing animosity or registering wrongs.

CHARLOTTE BRONTE

run with integrity,

Thou shalt not be a victim. Thou shalt not be a perpetrator. Above all, thou shalt not be a bystander.

HOLOCAUST MUSEUM,
Washington, D.C.

Dear children, let's not merely say that we love each other; let us show the truth by our actions.

1 JOHN 3:18 NLT

Superheroes always have a fatal flaw. They overlooked their own need to be saved. I try to keep this in mind when I begin thinking I'm Wonder Woman.

The roar of the approaching snowplow was like our personal starter gun. I was twelve and the protective sister. The rocky bank past our bus stop shelter allowed freedom to explore and escape the knowledge that alcoholism was strangling our family. I protected my sister from so much and there we were facing a snowplow moving faster than we were. I pushed her ahead, jumped and the plow obliviously drove by. Both of us buried by snow, our laughs echoed to a running neighbor who feared us dead. Honestly, for all my tension, I never felt more alive.

JULIE ARDUINI

run for those who need a champion,

run when no one else does.

All that you are seeking is also seeking you. If you lie still, sit still, it will find you. It has been waiting for you a long time.

CLARISSA PINKOLA ESTES

It was in a bathtub back in New York, reading Italian words aloud from a dictionary, that I first started mending my soul. My life had gone to bits and I was so unrecognizable to myself that I probably couldn't have picked me out of a police lineup. But I felt a glimmer of happiness when I started studying Italian, and when you sense a faint potentiality for happiness after such dark times you must grab onto the ankles of that happiness and not let go until it drags you face-first out of the dirt.

ELIZABETH GILBERT, *Eat, Pray, Love*

When my daughter was about seven years old, she asked me one day what I did at work. I told her I worked at the college—that my job was to teach people to draw. She stared back at me incredulous, and said, "You mean they forget?"

HOWARD IKEMOTO

. . . Is anyone happy? Let him sing songs of praise.

JAMES 5:13 NIV

run like happiness is within your grasp, run until it finds you.

 Happiness may be elusive, but we all have an inkling of the necessary ingredients to produce it. The question is what are those ingredients for you?

My friends are my estate.

EMILY DICKINSON

run with kindness and compassion, and the heart of a true friend.

Do all the good you can. By all the means you can. In all the ways you can. In all the places you can. At all the times you can. To all the people you can. As long as ever you can.

JOHN WESLEY

Kindness has always mattered to our father. He taught us to honor people, and he has encouraged us since before I can remember to empathize with human suffering. When I was a teenager he'd say, "Ann, go do something that helps people. Do something of service. It will always make you feel good about your life."

ANN CURRY

You gave me life and showed me kindness, and in your providence watched over my spirit.

JOB 10:12 NIV

 Women who get things done, help others and take care of themselves have all discovered that they need a team. Who is on your team?

run with your soul—full, run with a grateful spirit.

At night I would lie in bed and watch the show, how bees squeezed through the cracks of my bedroom wall and flew circles around the room, making that propeller sound, a high-pitched zzzzzz that hummed along my skin. I watched their wings shining like bits of chrome in the dark and felt the longing build in my chest. The way those bees flew, not even looking for a flower, just flying for the feel of the wind, split my heart down its seam.

SUE MONK KIDD, *The Secret Life of Bees*

"It's snowing still," said Eeyore gloomily. "So it is." "And freezing." "Is it?" "Yes," said Eeyore. "However," he said, brightening up a little, "we haven't had an earthquake lately."

A. A. MILNE, *The House at Pooh Corner*

Give thanks to the LORD, for he is good; his love endures forever.

1 CHRONICLES 16:34 NIV

The secret to gratefulness is to change your perspective.
Sometimes this may require standing on your head.

run without comparisons, celebrate your own brand of beauty.

During the summer I would run the six blocks home with books from the bookmobile stacked [precariously] in my arms. I was long-legged and skinny and I spent long hours on our front porch swing reading. At night I would read until I fell asleep. I read every one of those books. I never lost one or turned it in late. I still run, and I have a second-place trophy for a 10K. But my favorite memory is of the skinny ten-year-old, running to and from the bookmobile, discovering the world.

MARY ORNDORFF

We're all pretty, thankfully. It is a good thing to be pretty. But we are not just pretty, and pretty all by itself is not worth much since it lasts only about an hour, relative to the rest of your life.

JILL CONNER BROWNE,
The Sweet Potato Queens Book of Love

I'm a big woman. I need big hair.

ARETHA FRANKLIN

Instead, it should be that of your inner self, the unfading beauty of a gentle and quiet spirit, which is of great worth in God's sight.

I PETER 3:4 NIV

We are much more than the sum of our parts.

run with your genius and your imperfections, consider that perfection may be a flawed concept.

I like the fact that in ancient Chinese art the great painters always included a deliberate flaw in their work. Human creation is never perfect.

MADELEINE L'ENGLE

The thing that is really hard, and really amazing, is giving up on being perfect and beginning the work of becoming yourself.

ANNA QUINDLEN

Our deepest fear is not that we are inadequate. Our deepest fear is that we are powerful beyond measure. It is our light, not our darkness, that most frightens us. We ask ourselves: "Who am I to be brilliant, gorgeous, talented, fabulous?" Actually, who are you not to be?

NELSON MANDELA

Every good and perfect gift is from above . . .

JAMES 1:17 NIV

We all have genius, a place where God has touched us and left a piece of himself behind on purpose. Our job is to discover it.

run with verve and humor,
make peace with your expectations.

Things turn out best for the people who make

the best out of the way things turn out.

ART LINKLETTER

Just because things don't work out the way you planned them doesn't mean they didn't work out well.

ADAIR LAURA,
Normal Is Just a Setting on the Dryer

A wise woman builds her home, but a foolish woman tears it down with her own hands.

PROVERBS 14:1 NLT

Charlie Brown: *What can you do when you don't fit in? What can you do when life seems to be passing you by?*

Lucy: *Follow me. I want to show you something. (They get to the top of a hill.) See the horizon over there? See how big this world is? See how much room there is for everybody? Have you ever seen any other worlds?*

Charlie Brown: No.

Lucy: *As far as you know, this is the only world there is, right?*

Charlie Brown: Right.

Lucy: *There are no other worlds for you to live in, right?*

Charlie Brown: Right.

Lucy: *You were born to live in this world, right?*

Charlie Brown: Right.

Lucy: Well live in it then! *Five cents please.*

CHARLES SCHULZ, *Peanuts*

Every woman needs at least one friend that you can make laugh until tears run down her face and puddle on her upper lip.

run faster than the feet of
your enemy without—within—
run with the voice that applauds
the air you breathe.

Every morning in Africa, a gazelle wakes up. It knows it must outrun the fastest lion or it will be killed. Every morning in Africa, a lion wakes up. It knows it must run faster than the slowest gazelle, or it will starve. It doesn't matter whether you're a lion or gazelle. When the sun comes up, you'd better be running.

> attributed to ROGER BANNISTER shortly after running the first sub-4 mile

It took me a long time not to judge myself through someone else's eyes.

> SALLY FIELD

Do not judge, or you too will be judged.

> MATTHEW 7:1 NIV

In every woman's head there is the voice of a female saboteur. I call her the bad girlfriend, because if she were a real woman I would have nothing to do with her.

I believe that the
adrenaline that fear
produces is really our
body telling our head,
"Hey baby, I'm ready.
What's next?"

run like you are brave, even if your knees are shaking, run with a battle cry, and a song of your own.

You can't be brave if you've only had wonderful things happen to you.

MARY TYLER MOORE

Only when we are no longer afraid do we begin to live.

DOROTHY THOMPSON

I'm just the instrument for the song to do whatever it's supposed to do—heal, inspire or encourage. It's not all about me, it's about the song. I'm just the lucky girl who gets to sing these songs.

MARTINA MCBRIDE

She is clothed with strength and dignity; she can laugh at the days to come.

PROVERBS 31:25 NIV

It was my favorite time of day. Dinner was over, the dishes were done. My daddy would make his way to the corner of the living room. And the anticipation would mount as he sat down on the threadbare couch and picked up his favorite guitar. As he began to strum, he'd nod at me and the dance would begin. Round and round the living room I'd dance, no longer a four-year-old with skinned knees and pigtails. Round and round I'd twirl. My hair came loose; my daddy's eyes twinkled. And I knew that I could do and be anything that I could imagine. Because I was, after all, a princess.

KRISTEN HANSEN

run like the world depends on it.
run toward the arms of God.

I would rise before dawn, splash my face with water, and pull on my shorts, shirt and shoes. Somewhere in the process my hair would end up in a ponytail and a sweatshirt would be pulled on for protection against the chill. The rhythm of my shoes pounding the pavement and my steady breathing were the only sounds I could hear. It was my morning song and although my running shoes are long since retired, I can still feel the rush of the run whenever I close my eyes.

CINDEE SPARKS

Hope begins in the dark; the stubborn hope that if you just show up and try to do the right thing, the dawn will come. You wait and watch and work: You don't give up.

ANNE LAMOTT

Perseverance is failing nineteen times and succeeding the twentieth.

JULIE ANDREWS

For God did not give us a spirit of timidity, but a spirit of power, of love and of self-discipline.

2 TIMOTHY 1:7 NIV

 When we believe that we are on a mission entrusted to us alone, our lives come into focus.

run toward the mark and the horizon of purpose that stretches before you—waiting.

How we spend our days is, of course, how we spend our lives.

ANNIE DILLARD

Give her the reward she has earned, and let her works bring her praise at the city gate.

PROVERBS 31:31 NIV

A horizon is like being given a new canvas with an array of brand-new paints and brushes. After you get over the rush and anticipation you must begin the work of deciding what you will paint.

I love more than anything to be outside, walking. Even now, I must get outside, daily, to see the sky. Maybe it comes from the fact that I grew up in northern Montana on a wheat farm and I was constantly outside, even in the cold. Off to the west were the rugged Rockies and stretched overhead was the Big Sky. I remember one day, one crystallized moment when I was ten—not an extraordinary day, yet as I walked outside under the sky, I felt so alive, so filled with belief that anything was possible.

NANCIE CARMICHAEL

run to rescue, to reinvent,

run to lay claim to the girl in you.

Over the years I have developed a picture of what a human being living humanely is like. She is a person who understands, values and develops her body, finding it beautiful and useful; a person who is real and is willing to take risks, to be creative, to manifest competence, to change when the situation calls for it, and to find ways to accommodate to what is new and different, keeping that part of the old that is still useful and discarding what is not.

VIRGINIA SATIR

Life loves to be taken by the lapel and told: "I'm with you kid. Let's go."

MAYA ANGELOU

run like a girl

Because you've always stood up for me, I'm free to run and play.

I hold on to you for dear life, and you hold me steady as a post.

PSALM 63:5,6, *The Message*

run like a girl

It is never too late to be what you might have been.

GEORGE ELIOT

run like a girl

To unpathed waters, undreamed shores.

WILLIAM SHAKESPEARE

run like there's nothing better than to run like a girl.

This is the only race worth running. I've run hard right to the finish, believed all the way.

2 TIMOTHY 4:7 *The Message*

This is just the beginning...

Running like a girl is a metaphor for the woman who moves within the rhythm of her own authentic life. It is the call to stop looking outside yourself and discover what God has already sealed in your identity and to do the work of championing the passion and purpose God placed inside you.

The purpose of this book is to help you step back, breathe in, and connect to the big picture for your life. What do you see? What would make you excited about tomorrow? What do you dream of? Tell us more...let us be part of your fan club at www.runlikeagirl.org. This is a safe, judgment-free place for you to tell us your story, gather your energies and begin to consider what comes next.

The world is waiting...

KATHY VICK,
Certified Life Coach

MAY 1961

Kathy Vick is a Certified Life Coach, author and speaker. She has worked in Christian publishing since 1981 and has directed and contributed to multiple projects including Christian magazines, radio, websites, and family seminars.

Kathy has written and published articles, essays, and sidebars for women since 1995. She is the author of *Lessons in Buoyancy: Letting go of the Perfect Proverbs 31 Woman.* She is the cocreator of the Mom2Mom gift book series and author of *7 Reasons to Be Grateful You're the Mother of a Blended Family.* She is the founder of www.runlikeagirl.org, a website that supports and inspires women who are in a place of starting something new or starting over.

Things that delight Kathy: road trips with her husband, laughing with her kids, and days in her calendar reserved for girlfriends. Kathy lives in Portland, Oregon, with her husband, Pat, and her retriever, Carmella. She is the mother of two grown children, Patrick and Andrea.

www.runlikeagirl.org